METHOD & MADNESS

E. Martin Pedersen

Published by Ensorcellia,
an imprint of Odyssey Books, in 2024

www.odysseybooks.com.au

A Cataloguing-in-Publication entry is available
from the National Library of Australia

ISBN: 978-1922311580 (pbk)
ISBN: 978-1922311597 (ebook)

Cover image: Soul Nebula, NASA/JPL-Caltech/UCLA

Everywhere I go, I find a poet has been there before me.

– attributed to Sigmund Freud

CONTENTS

SUPEREGO

MELANCHOLIA

PHANTASY

EGO

ETIOLATE BLUES

That man sitting in my chair near the window
Reading the same page of *Naked Lunch* over and over
Wondering, if anything, how much longer his socks will last
How many more pairs of socks he will need

Turns to look out at nothing, although the sky is right there
What is he doing sitting in my chair? Spying?
On a brilliant Sunday morning at 11 am
After making tea and drinking it, which he can't remember

Social Learning theorists say that self-pity is a common
method for gaining attention
So that must be the African violet's game
That feeble houseplant his mother gave him
That never got enough light, never got enough

It won't thrive, neither will it die in San Francisco
Living alone is no surprise but a point of shy pride
Last April they gave a pride parade and everyone showed
Except the sitter and the window cat who jumps into his lap

Not for love, just the warmth of a human body
And what little light streams in on them from above.

COMING OUT OF THE COMA

It's a week or ten or a month or ten years
My God. Come quick! It's a miracle, he returns.

Hi everybody, what time is it? Take me home. Drive.

New decade, new pres, let's see, Rowan and Martin still on?
The *viva la raza* mural on the side of the movie theater's
still there
though flaking badly,.
Sno-White Drive-In became a Chicken Shack.
The Mall, still its little planet – Starship Enterprise – looks
smaller now, seedy
With the Forgiveness Church across the street – they never
move churches
big old trees in front gone.
University still houses the library
Ruben's librarian with the braid still at the front desk?
Man, I'd like to check her out,
like I checked out this book on parallel universes.

Have you seen my parents lately?
Is my brother still mad at me
over that silly misunderstanding with his wife?
That retarded guy in middle school who knew everything
about Italian racing bikes.

I bet my erector-set nephew's not a kid anymore,
baseball player maybe.
Is my dog, Lucy, okay?
I don't see anyone I know here.

Am I slipping, slipping back in?
Another ticket to ride, back
Back to the other side of the worm hole,
In and out of the coma with a passport and
Luggage coming out
In, out.

AVOIDING MIRRORS

My daydreams and nightmares have the same plot
with different protagonists or the same
people from my past life passed over on the other shore
people (see above for their real names) showing up on my doorstep
        now that I finally have a doorstep
the horror and the joyous pathos
Wither they show up or not they do
in the playhouse up here
torment me as a hint
as to after many, many years
I need to step out of the bath of my past self and stories
face the mirror
wipe off the clouds
not be afraid.

PUNCTUATION

I choose the question mark and the exclamation point
You can have all the others
Give up my whole life, home and family, for a stranger
We had bliss, we had six weeks of perfect happiness
He'd run into 7-11 in Tennessee for breakfast
yelling something to me from across the highway
Without looking, he stepped in front of a truck.
I'll pay for those six weeks
I'll remember every second
the glow, the bounce
I still swell; I still ache
You have a peaceful home life, which
I will never have and will always envy
but then, you can't even imagine
? !

JUMPING IN AND OUT OF THE MIRROR

Against myself I bump heads
while pulling the drifting continents together with rope
If I let go
they float apart in mirrors
staving, pleased with my image of suffering, into my hands ...
She told me her sister had been murdered, but it was a lie
        pulling me up like an anchor
to believe her suffering could also be mine
I just want
– like a baserunner in game seven –
to get home
sprinting at reflective hoops, quicksilver hurdles
and a peyote woman of my own choosing
like coyote
Retracing my steps through the multiplicious crossroads
on a round planet
in one dimension
after another.

SEATED AFTER LUNCH

The shifting shadows of tree branches
on the ground
waltz (one two three, one two three)
with patches of brilliant March sun
while this wind chills
behind my right ear.

I bet that woman has soft skin ...

Time for me to get
up from this park bench again.

AM I BREATHING GAS?

As our bus rolls down the street on the right, there's a
terribly long connected block of three-story houses, and
in the big plate glass window of the second story of each
house, there's a black man, a young black man, in each
window looking down on our road, and I look up at the
mountain off to the left in the distance; I ask the others of
course what it could mean, what it could mean is – we've
been given an assignment
to go sleep on that mountain.

We follow the road to the top
then a green storm of light green lightning and green clouds
of light on the silent mountain top eerie us out
I say we pull into a closed gas station to go ask the open
next-door grocer
who, untroubled, explains the green light every night –
change of plans.

We pull into the closed car wash
for safety and curious lustiness
as she sits on my lap, I raise her dress and rub my hands up
and down her legs, she wants to know, *what are you doing?*

We go to the Shakespeare bookstore, in the side door, to the
back room of discount books

the marriage is celebrated, but I stay after and buy lots of
very important books.
We don't go up on the mountain but stay in town wondering
that no one knows – the green mist of apathy – the press
doesn't care enough to write the story, I try but can't
I even begin going up on the mountain, but find nothing
there except the green lights from a different angle.

And the sewer backs up in our shack and tons of junk pass by
on a conveyor belt
I take some curios and go back to my hiker friends and
my lover to propose going up on the mountain with no
enthusiasm or conviction left.

My hair is uncontrollable
white pigeons peck at the dirt
one boot lace is untied.

WATCHING THROUGH A HOLE IN THE FENCE

What does he want?
What gives him joy?
Where is he focused?
What does he fear?

I want to help you
Not everyone improves
I'm a skilled artist
Doing what I do.

A hole in the fence
I'm not at the prom
When I say, I love you
Be aware I'm wrong.

Watching the big game
But not joining in
I might get fondled
Might commit sin.

To play
The game
That way.

WHITE LIGHTNING

Stunning white light
tracing the veins
in my tired eyes
in my blinking brain
flashing jaggedy vertical/horizontal
the roots of an old tree
tree of knowledge perhaps
or rather the knowledge of good and evil
or the temptation of evil, that is
or the snake behind Adam's leaf
lined like an open hand
that Eve might bite.

I watch the storm
transfixed
white shapes impressing the retina
fading soon but remaining somehow
charging lightning fast through the system
eye to brain
then beyond, then gone –
like the first time
I drank moonshine
I did squawk
what else?
like the first before

I saw you
giving me the shock I needed
to jumpstart my heart
to boom and roar.

WAITING FOR WHAT IN THE BANK

It's cold in the bank
the metal desks marble floor
beige walls plastic plants humid papers
cold drinking fountain
aluminum elevator
chilly computer screens
cold hard cash
(you were waiting for me to say that)
and the people who enjoy their work
the guiding principle of pre and post-theft
the air conditioning on high so
it can't be hell, hell would be hella warmer.

I'm waiting in the bank
where they keep so much
I've been here five minutes or maybe
my whole life
long time
waiting
waiting in the bank of treasures
for redemption
forgiveness
charity
pity.

ID

GOING TO THE EDGE OF THE LAND

We drove and drove, taking rest under blond Australian
weeds
the comfort station had a toilet but no running water, hold it
no coffee   no ice cream
ample apologies: "I know you're not from here,"
said the ashamed young woman. "It's not always this bad."
(we are from here, everywhere is here, everywhere is bad)
our sandwiches were good though
eaten by the monastery watching butterflies
until a Vespa drove us away with its buzz
onwards out toward the edge.

The decision made itself; no amount of my worrying could
stop us now
we drove down dirt country roads twisted like treesnakes
backtracking from tail to head
through card-playing villages and go-home rentals
in the stuffy midafternoon we found it –
the vision from on high among the ruins
the glaringly irreal parking area
past it all, sturdy and calm we walked
out to the lakes where tiny boys captured tiny fish for the
aquarium
and the trail got soft
Look, this mountain has a hole.

no time for a game on the guano white checkerboard
Don't Look Back
walk clear to the tightrope between everything and eternity
it's always closer than you think
as we slowly melted into sugary sun tea
and talked of house construction.

I will never forget that bath
dipped in gold lifelikenessless
the laughter of gravity towels
finding ourselves as we knew each other
seventeen years ago
grown   tingling   holding hands
back on Sicilian sand.

ONE SWELTERING DAY ON THE CARONTE

The short man's five rigid fingers shot energy rays
Then his hands went back into his curly hair for lubrification
Then his fingers became erect again and shot more
frustration juice
He bit his marble hand, bent way over, and yelled and cried
(not real tears though, don't confuse acting with acting)
In any case, I couldn't hear a sound locked in my glass
observation booth.

I did get to see the girls going at it, five or six of them
Heads down like rams, flailing
Pulling shocks of hair, slapping faces, breaking glasses
(females know no rules)
One had a switch for herding goats
And *everybody* crept up to see the show, gratis, and kibitz.

Except the northern gentleman in the next car with the
yellow shirt and red tie
He didn't get out either, clicking his tongue (animals!)
Won't somebody exercise some authority here?
Where's the captain, in the wine cellar?
I realized as we pulled up to Messina and the lazy peace
officers came aboard

That I was a northerner too and would never grow accustomed
To this welcome home.

Included – in a family not my own –
I am held in fond regard or perhaps hostage
Bondage but not blood
Blood forgives
Blood washes, they say here
You don't know what a blood is, I say
Unless you went to my high school
And stayed out of the bathrooms at my high school
I won't go into that because
I know you can't understand
Around a mourning table of Sicilian focaccia
Washed down with American Co'Cola
Cousins remember the rusty go-carts and funny mini-bikes of their speedy youth
The same stories told at each funeral
So that I almost feel like I was there then
But no, this isn't my family, I wasn't there
I have been adopted as a houseplant
A philodendron, tall and common
While I fancy throwing other rocks
Into other rivers with other kids
Drinking and eating other stuff
[Beverly cream soda and Moon pies]
I don't belong here

Any more than a eucalyptus tree outside Oz
Or Adam outside the garden, that is
So why am I here?

We are all destined in eventual generations
To exile
The either-or's-stay-leave's always leave someday
For their 50 miles of elbow room
And that can't be taken back (no do-overs)
I left
My fault
I left
As you will sooner or later
And lost I don't know what
And gained I don't know what
How could you?
How could I?
Only that the lust for peculiarity
Means my grandchildren will call this weird place
Home
When they leave it
On that same ferry.

LA SOLUZIONE DEL FIAMMIFERO [THE MATCH SOLUTION]

We have a personnel problem here
they won't pay us overtime anymore
we've had three strikes in the last month
it's so damn hot who gives a shit and
we have three carloads of mail here
that we just cannot and will not move.

In Catania, Sicily, Italy, 1981, three train-carloads of mail
lost alphabet souls
up
in
smoke.

Dear Diana sorry about your father passing
Dear Signor Jones your tax rebate this year amounts to
Dear Dr. Smith your presence is requested at a job interview
Dear Rita will you marry me
Dear Mr. Vonnegut we will gladly publish your book, we liked
the part about
so it goes.

PALMYRA REMEMBERED

Alone in the ruins of a city left
walking the streets listening to the ghastly ululation
these stiff columns and walls and pavement here
are why I came so far into the desert;
other cities fell and were taken
down, apart, and put back together
new cities on the old
legos.

Why spend weekdays and weekends chipping stone
and then leave it useless in its place?
move it over here and I'll make my house from it
I like recycling, it's clean, it imitates nature.

You see them walking the avenue
growing old, making love, being born again
carried in and out of doors.

The last fifteen years of my life
have been dedicated
to memorizing the history of my kin folk
caulking the dike, so to speak
standing with few others placing heavy blocks of stone in
the shallows
to hold back the sea, preserve the shore

beautiful blocks stolen from the ruins
when it seems that everyone else wants to bury them
to make ugly new houses above.

They might be right
but if the old city disappears
where will the ghosts sleep tonight?

BUMMING A THIRD-CLASS TRAIN

The Germ Theory of disease
goes out the stuck-open window
of a third-class train
Luxor to Cairo
in a cloudy glass of Nile water
passed around like a bong in a dorm
by grinning gentlemen in dresses
then sleeping curled like a doe
on a tottering wood bench
back to the oasis, where I need to go.

KING HUSSEIN AND THE BLIND MAN

We recycled all the alphabet into illiterate soup
so I can't go back
over Jordan
through three feet of stacked news
and read the subdued headlines
(of a week or so ago)
but I do remember King Hussein
carrying his dusty nation into the age of Aquarius
making peace with his hands, inscrutably
dealing high stakes poker.
I wonder who cried, if anyone
looking at that photo
but if you've been there
if you've had your shoes x-rayed
had every page of every book flipped
if you've gotten the correct stamps and photos with great
difficulty
and know the river's real width, depth, breadth, volume …

Underneath
the same page
I remember a picture
of a quiet middle-aged blind man
retired switchboard jockey maybe from Baltimore
and the story

of a new operation procedure
some science stuff
that gave him that TV moment
of taking off the blindfold
and seeing for the first time
in his life
seeing.

He may not have it easy from now on
I wouldn't know,
sight is such an anxious gift
and, well,
any kind
of peace
is a miracle.

MOVING STILL

one house
with one chair
ingenious invention
to keep legs at 90°
it is my house
my chair, my view
my rest, my energy
solid down through the legs all
to the center of the earth
through to California
lifted by a twister
the up and at 'em
gyroscope

MISS AMERICA

If you can't read
you could miss America
you might drive right by
If it really is
as the billboards say
there's a good excuse
for a sale today
drive-in, suck-'em-in sale
happy meal: happy price
recliner sale
Sit back relax and buy buy baby goodbye
convertible sale
software
overshoes
the Bahamas

When all goes well
Babies are safe
From harms
Alarms
In arms
My God, how the money rolls in

But then you die
Open your fist

don't be surprised
to find
lilies $4.79 a dozen
and a brochure
on the family plan
at the Happy Valley Cemetery:
kids
          fly
                free

SUPEREGO

REMISSION OF CANCER

A fish laying on a slab of concrete
gasping like a warehouse on fire
strapped to a bed, smothered with a pillow
blackness pressing right on the eyeballs
fight panic while the boat fills, pointlessly
the pressure and fatigue of water.

Running a race with Jackie, from the car
across the wide green grass in the sparkling park
plenty of eucalyptus shade and reeds
down by the lake with the ducks and blond dogs
her open shirt shows her thick pink exclamation mark
we hold hands and giggling run our hearts out.

I KISSED YOU

I kissed you during the earthquake
I knew it wasn't right
But at that moment we were alive
And crouched together all that night

Under a table covered with debris
Later we'll search for our loved ones
I want to touch lips, close my eyes
Feel your strong back and buns

You kissed me during the earthquake
And all during the aftershocks
My shyness veil came down then
Along with entire city blocks.

CHARLENE'S GOLF BALL STORY

Charlene lived on the 17th hole
        I guess that's possible
she had a cat
that untrained would walk out onto the golf course
and steal balls
approach the green on 17
as the kids giggled as
kitty fetched Wilson Topflite one by one
under the fence into the yard.
The balls were kept in a bucket and one day
        when the bucket was full
some fat cigarman sliced one
over near them tricksters
Charlene and her sisters
looking through knotholes
they threw the whole bucket out onto the course
of course.

A CENTURY OF ACCUMULATION

Back when doubt
wasn't a way of life
Back in the one-song-per-person days
the die-standing-up days
survival of the meanest or luckiest
to follow the shining road
to goodies after passage
watch your husband's beard grow
hear the washing flap the line
no categories
no meteorology
no playing cards
Granddad in Seward, Alaska Territory
kept his family in a tent
covered twenty feet high with snow
all winter seven sons and a daughter
on elk and brown bear
hide shoes, potbelly stove
fishbone toothpicks
and the Holy Bible
chopping eternal wood
alongside Teddy Roosevelt.

What difference
solitaire and/or self-expression
If peace of mind
pursueth not
what love is really
what life is really
couched in billions of stars
we can't keep count
billions of T-shirts
billions of options
reflex emotions
we're buried alive
crushed under the cadavers
growing soft
unable to cough
we have too much
we have it all
except what
they had –
not all.

ME AND THE BEAST

Yes, when the beast sat across from me in the waiting room
I hated her
when I realized I was infected too
when we made love and she was inside me
our collusion began
now she scares me precisely
because she shadows me.

in the marked-off square of a provincial capital between the city hall and the
        cathedral
there's a festival, colored lights and streamers
orange drink and sweetcorn under a black sky-roof
two boys hold my palms, their father my friend drifted away with the flotsam
cherry bombs go off, rockets straight up and down onto tight-as-matchheads
men start laughing and howling
nurses cannot get through to the fainted and burned
drunks fight with their claws like cats in a barrel
cops cannot reach them and they begin to fight
everyone I see's drunk and fighting, hurt and bleeding
housewives, neighbors, English teachers, Roman Catholics
bombs and rockets, screaming and burning skin, embers falling like confetti

the church roof is on fire
but we cower in its locked doorway anxiously unable to get home

in the stuffy open quadrant where the roads intersect before the huge mosque
pushed around by people at a party, come on, it's a holiday, holy day
cartwheels and chickpeas, clapping and chanting
everyone's happy, pushing, singing *Carnival in Rio* and *the Beer Barrel Polka*
pious men in a dimly lit room whirling away the night
we see them twirl from outside in their elegant wine-color dresses and pill-box hats
outside too are virtuous people, they do not steal
except one man in a thousand, screaming in terror
when the nine hundred nighty-nine shout, "Get him, thief!"
he's broken the law, you see, we must bring him to justice
thousands of long arms grab at him like living jungle vines, like flesh-eaters
as he madly shoots right past my shoulder
and his animal eyes beg for mercy he will not get

in the ring around the diamond
a tiered coliseum where gladiators meet – all ticking
everyone knows the true meaning of "Strike!" "Steal!" "Charge!"

keeping us on the brink as we sit back down, stand up,
sing out
hotdog wrappers and seagulls spin above the field
if we were just a little warmer, I'm afraid
I'm afraid when we yell, when *I* yell, louder than the rest,
more convinced sounding
BEAT LA, I hate LA, don't wear blue, we won't traffic with you
BEAT LA down the next block
we are the righteous gang of colors orange and black
standing tall in a Mr. Clean judgment pose, we growl out our
human growth hormones
Yes! Yes!
Yet where is the advantage in kicking a man when he's down,
beating the weaker opponent?
frankly we are disgusted by the dust devil that broke out of
the cage and ripped and
        beat LA and busted through all the windows –

        and still somehow

let the light and the fresh air in

OUR WAR IS OVER

As Melanie said, "There's nothing nicer than an unnecessary
peace song."

Fear-weary *niños* jumping at the Indochina *piñata*
Rooftop chopper finale folly
Brimming holy roller arks
yet to embark
just the latest fad
impressed
by CBS.

We didn't know where that tension came from
until it went away.

In a California forest sanctuary
we stood with our comrades priests teachers brothers and
sisters
in a harmony circle with our arms entangled, crossed in front,
joined beside
patches of snow on the ground
some heads up, some down,
eyes open/closed, breathing normally
humming
praise for pacifism.

Our developmentally impaired childhood finally complete:
You can sleep now, Jim Morrison.

COLONOSCOPY

Shine your light
Shine your little light
Shine your little light on me

I'll have an evacuation cocktail, please
one part rotten fish heads
one part swamp water
a dash of copper mine trailings
shaken not stirred
then I'd like to sit down please
sometimes I feel like
an exploding sack of
s. ampersand hashtag t. exclamation mark
so, explode man, share, out of control, guts everywhere
then later, when I'm tired of all that
fed up (I wish)
I'll lie on my left side
and watch television
Discovery Channel
        Hey look, that's me
        I'm a little star.

IN COURT

everyone tingles
marble columns open
their eyes to watch
the sweat gland welcome
pace and chat nothings
the electrons in the hardback law books
bounce out of the glass case
ricochet across the air of guilt
through the white coffee of
letter-number codes
even the three monkeys read clearly
with labored scansion
the Yahtzee dice
roll them now
four of a kind is not
enough, darling.

BEING CHASED

The Dogs of Hell, orange with black donut spots and orange glass eyes. They're on my trail. I look up and their slobber teeth shine in the twilight on all sides. If I run, they'll attack, no escape, no cover; if I stand, they'll attack too. They will bring me down like a football team and rip off my flesh like a kid opening Christmas presents.

I'm digging through the sand for my shadow who's suffocating underneath. When the sand slides back in the hole, hour glass-style, I am doomed, surrounded, trapped by the grains; there are hundreds, coming nearer, growing larger, famished, furious. They will go for my throat and genitals first.

In high water, rough choppy seas, no order to the waves. The water's gone berserk and lost itself shaking in panic – thousands of people mingling in a crowded railway station who don't go TO the trains or TO the exit, just sway and slosh for no reason surrounded by marble columns and cigarette machines, closed gates. Can't they see how desperate their plight is? Why don't they fight to get out, to see the horizon, to breathe clean air?

I am blind now, I hear only crashes, my spinning legs carry me nowhere. A sea hand puts its fingers through my ribs to squeeze the blood out of my heart. I am drowning in this chaos storm; they've won; I'm finished. Underwater, things are even worse.

I AM THE URGE TO SIGN MY NAME

I am coincidentally standing in the same spot as my body
reading the list of coffees in foreign script
the sandwich boy calls me "Bro" though my real name is
"Grumpy"
I must choose between cheddar, Jack, and Swiss
I can choose, I do
I am articulate, wielding semiotic influence
to make the sandwich girl laugh, I say "Brussels sprouts"
See? I am not a ghost.

I am wealthy, this cup warming my hands belongs to me
(not to the sunburnt man on the curb)
its tension becomes my tension
as I wheel off to meet blondes, eddies, corridors, Buddhists,
seabirds, metaphors, fogbanks
I make a contract with myself –
That's how important I am.

I am the tight string that over the years will bend the
cellist's fingers
As always cello, listener, and song.

MELANCHOLIA

GOOD FRIEND ON A BEACH

Was I not a good enough friend?
I just saw you the other day
and we laughed and drank
If I could have helped you
I had the keys to your house here on Maui
but you'd disappeared
After a week the police found you
on a secluded beach
a bullet in your brain
a note from the hospital
folded in your breast pocket
All bad news
You never were the patient sort.

I'm so sorry
You had to dot your 'i's
alone
And thank you
for being
Good friend.

DEATH OF A SENTIENT BEING

In the end, he died
he began foaming at the mouth
eyes flipped up
none of his family knew
what the hell to do
a neighbor woman sat on the floor
held his head like the Madonna
as all stood around watching
him finally shut up

refuse to say hello when we meet in the stairs
I loudly repeat myself up into his hideous smirk
I talk to him a lot actually
explain why he is so nauseating
I try to rehabilitate him
coerce him into obedience
threaten him with legal action (oooh, that'll scare him)
I threaten him with violence
lots of violence (I break his nose so easily blood gushes)
I spit on him and all, on their graves, his ancestors
leave him for last, torture and slowly cut off limbs
until he's all gone, screams of agony echo during the work
I'm sorry he's made me do
I saw that in a movie

but tenant meetings involve other people
horning in on our intimacy
they bitch about him too
almost as strongly as I do or more, I hold my tongue
others hate him as strongly as I do
but he is closer to me, next door
he is mine
I hear him walking in the house he stole by fraud
I hear him slam the door – blam, like a cherry bomb
in the middle of the night
like the door of the foreign legion fort, Fort Alamo
awaiting the final attack –
death and defeat await
as he skids his furniture about on tile
clanging into the clanging night

so, my question is, the question is:
is it proper etiquette
to thank the one
who taught you to hate
who channeled and strengthened
your natural rage
is this maturity
having enemiesa blessing disguised
and low?

ASBESTOS FACTORY

My friend's thin father
wore a tie with his cardigan
owned an asbestos factory
when we met, he said
"I didn't know."
I didn't understand
he said he'd owned an asbestos factory
and cried
"I didn't know."
no one blamed him or yes they did
an investigation held
he was absolved, innocent under the law
he really didn't know
yet he died shortly afterwards
from heartbreak and bleeding ulcers
thin well-dressed man
leaving me to repeat
"He didn't know."

HEIRLOOMS

Everybody's throwing heirlooms off the wagons
too much weight for the ox
one could sink on a river crossing
buy new trinkets at the gift shops
souvenirs from national parks concessionaires
or Chinese goods filling colorful discount stores
I still have a couple cute knickknacks
from Grandmother's home in Concord
paperweights, letter openers, the dog ashtray with his big mouth open
I asked the kids, who wants this old stuff when I'm dead?
they yelled, "Not us!"

I WAS DEAD

I was dead
        but I could still see
I saw blue skies
        and I waited for the crash sound
It didn't come, only a bump
        then I was born
You held me so gently
        my only feeling was fortune
I slept against your skin
        warm and fragrant like toast
Every day someone watching out for me
        for a change
For the first time –

Delicious new life of wonder
        and to think
I was dead.

CALL FOR PRAYER

Layla, you got me on my knees
I heard your call for prayer
Don't have a recurrence, please

My heart would grip and seize
Because it isn't fair
Layla, you got me on my knees

Layla, you deserve this the least
You had such lovely hair
Don't have a recurrence, please

Always healthy, fighting the beast
They say we get what we can bear
Layla, you got me on my knees

You're an artist, someone we need
I wish your pain I could share
Don't have a recurrence, please

Always loving, not consumed by greed
I don't want you to go anywhere
Layla, you got me on my knees
Don't have a recurrence, please
Layla.

WE WILL ALL BECOME VEGETARIANS

Unless we die first
Then we'll feed the wiggly carnivores
All those Fruit Loops make sweet meat
Unless cremation becomes obligation
And the dust joins smoke and arsenic
From the mines where we bore
To force milk from a dry teat
Unless everything runs on solar wind and wave
Such simple energy can do so much
Drive cross country on a dime
Live a century on a dollar
Unless we abolish money
And just give it all away
You need shoes – here
I'd like coconut pie – here
What a wonderful ...
Unless we die first.

I REPEAT REPEAT

I repeat myself, repeat myself
Every time the same, over and over again
Walk the same empty corridor
By the same locked doors
Breathe in and out
All the chords in my new song are the same
As the chords in my old song; is this a game?
I ate chocolate cake last week; I enjoyed it
I bought another one this week
Sex they say should be different every time
I wouldn't know, I wouldn't know
Is redundancy such a crime?

Then I noticed that I begin brushing
With the teeth on top front then to the left
Then right, then bottom teeth
Lastly in back and on the tops, edges
Gums and tongue
Every freaking time
A million days in a row
Well, not a million anymore –
Oh, I just thought of something
I will only do once.

ON REVIEW

You die
then you get a year to reflect
then a review session
– What? –
I wish I hadn't always wanted the latest fashion
that seems such a waste now
and smoking
though there was pleasure
all that buying, burning
lighting, discarding butts
quite a pastime
maybe I could have done better, been better
without maybe

all I left were my kids
and they barely knew me
they threw out my love letters and souvenirs

so, it's all senseless then you die?
on review, I don't know.

PHANTASY

THE KOI ARE NOT INDIFFERENT

They see us
They crack jokes
They think my belly flops
They snicker and click their tongues
That I need a shave
That you should brush your teeth
That we look cute on the couch.

Valerie talks to the fish
Who would answer back.

The big orange ones think Jeopardy is dumb
But the white speckled ones all enjoy Beavis and Butthead
(there's no accounting for tastes)
They don't, however, laugh out loud.

Valerie understands their silence.

The sound of one fin clapping
I've listened for all my life
and I thought I was deaf
until the words came from Valerie,
Two hands clapped
with a crashing snappy slap
and I realized

she was right:
The koi are not indifferent.

WAITING FOR THE BUS

Why don't poets talk about the bus?
The people on the bus
The bus breaking down
Looking out the window of the bus
Waiting for the bus
                                        that never will come,
We stood, it wasn't right
they'd switched the lines
they're always switching lines
and told no one
you just had to know.
We didn't, so we waited
watching the trees and tourists
gum on the concrete sidewalk
felt our sore feet
didn't speak
the ignorant ones
those left behind
losers

How can that chain-smoking man still be alive?
Or the ugly scowling woman, sister stole her man
that pissed-off kid who can't speak the language correctly.

By what right?
out of six billion cogs
chipping on the really big wheel

The prostitute's well-dressed
clients, for instance
her only friends
guests at her wedding
to the priest's bastard son
the blue-eyed bus driver.
I look them over, their greasy hair
honestly, I want them all dead
Samson, bring down the house
Hulk, crush the crowded bus
Steamroller, clear the street, comin' through.
Otherwise what fun I'm missing,
I could almost kill myself
here waiting

for the bus never came,

We never got on
never went home
never got out of the cold
never had supper
and a soft bed
a human touch
ever.

LOOK THE OTHER WAY

I rode an elevator
with my ex-wife
and never said a word
We've become good actors
theatre abba absurd
Or proof, old dogs
new tricks learned
Yet my back then
returned and burned
Multiple personality dis-order
The mystery of the sphincter
leaves a single doubt
Who was that man I saw me with
in the looking-glass so strung out?

I turned away
Christ, I couldn't watch that
Bosnia, May 17, 1993
Somebody brought war dead back
to their families in plastic trash bags
and the TV news had the poor judgment to show
the wool shawl women opening presents
the black rotted flesh, the stench
One old hag held a skull to her own head and sang her
laments

with the other arm she beat her chest and cried dry tears
Then another truck of peek-a-boo bones pulled up
I turned away.

I can't explain to you this mechanism in another way
When you get into "you-don't" mode
teetering on the fulcrum like a Road Runner rock
and you're unloved, unappreciated, unwanted
desperate for mercy and pity, taunted
I know what you mean, I know what you want
I want to give you what you want
but I don't; I give you what you need
the cold shoulder, the silent treatment
you wake up screaming, "More!"
I look the other way.

DO FOOD

I'd do food with you
Let's do food together
Okay, let's do it –
Weave spaghetti
Bounce a meatball
Ski down parmesan mountain
Fill the ocean with pistachio wine
Ride a celery stalk onto the burlesque stage
Pick your teeth with a coffee bean
Land in a bowl of lizards and lettuce
Tasty gumdrops stuck up your nose
Butterscotch pudding between our toes –
I'd only do
food with you.

It's not the food, it's the thought of food
all a matter of ideas, see?
it's not the sex/death/art, it's the idea of sex/death/art
well, and the act
the lick, the chew
me and you
do food.

DRIVING MY WAY

Sometimes I coolly let you
ram in front of me,
cut me off,
endanger us both,
other times I don't.
I'm not following a personal rule
cannot tell you beforehand
you'll be able to tell
if not, don't dare
I may not be good today
I may feel pressed, traffic-trapped.
I am Mr. Nice Guy
but I drive my way.

WEAKNESS

My chick and I had a child
And named it Silence
It required no uneasy sex
Over the milk
Not brought from the store
That and all the rest
Your thin long legs
Now seem like brittle sticks
Those I longed to press
If I only had
A new Gibson guitar
My humiliation would pass
Or the teenager
At the donut shop
In fiction she's not innocent
Until with her child
She yells, "Silence!"
And I hush myself up next
I cannot win
If this fate I possess
Ends in a jumbled mess
Of weakness.

THE GOSPEL ACCORDING TO BOB

Jesus drummed his fingers on the table at the last supper
He drummed his fingers there
He looked from side to side
Ran his fingers through his hair.

Jesus spilled the red wine on the white tablecloth at the last supper
It left a nasty stain
Which didn't bother him
He knew he wouldn't drink again.

Mary screamed and broke down along the pathway to Golgotha
It all felt so unreal
Her baby got strung up
All she could do was kneel.

Peter leaned against a wall down an alley in Jerusalem
He wished he were back home
He smoked a cigarette
Smelled of fish and catacombs.

Jesus blinked away blood under his new hat of roses
He liked to hurt like hell
He danced under the cross
Will he ever ring the bell?

Elvis was the King so we crucified him on Good Friday
Hung his velvet portrait too
His suit sent out to clean
Love me tender, love me true.

THE SUN KNOWS I'M A FOOL

I wait for the sun to call the role
And pass the mail at breakfast
I need a word from Dearest John
So I can face certain death.

Tie me to the chain gang
Let me work the roads
My balloon will fly alone
As only you should know.

Drink a cup of liquor
Poison to my meat
Drink a cup of laughter
Till I stop to breathe.

If magic had been my major
I'd deliver you to me
But today the sun is saying
You snipped my thread, I'm free.

PHOTOS OF FOOD

So many photos of food
So many photos of food
Can we eat the photos?
If I send them to Africa or Alaska
If I send you a photo of food
are you nourished?
Warm and dry inside
or envious as ice
of my delicious
food and you
only get a frozen photo.

Yet when food is gone
photos remain.

THE PERSUADERS

Oh the match
the little finger of soft wood with the colored cap
the fire inside bursts with gladness
when released, the genie
the wish, burn burn burn
twigs and sticks and logs
paper, blank or printed
an entire house, an entire life's work
did Ellison's second man become invisibly hot
the match, Ras the destroyer
needs intention, needs the push of evil
to explode with hell.

Oh the bullet
the little penis-head of brass and lead
the hole maker, the nothing maker
says I'll make some nothing right here
I'll enter this brand-new virgin hole
pull the hole in after me
I'll let light shine inside
this flesh, this red meat
of a boy or girl innocent
it's not my fault
I'll defy hope

squirt for me, I am the finalizer
the teeter balances on my stiff tip.

Oh the ball-point pen

THE NAME OF GOD

> *"'God' is an ambiguous word in our language because it appears to refer to something that is known. But the transcendent is unknowable and unknown. God is transcendent, finally, of anything like the name 'God'."*
> *– Joseph Campbell*

Oh, to drop the name
drop the name, drop the name
Oh, to drop the name

Kissing up
Kissing up
to God
to get in good
so God
will remember
your name
when it's time.

Fall on your knees
Fall on your knees
on the bathroom rug
before the porcelain altar

Fall on your knees
in a crowded ballroom
That's the "*grand geste*"
pretend to pray, who's to know?
go on fool
thyself

Brahman
Aten
Mother Earth
Jehovah
Krishna
Allah
Baha

Stand in the corner
Face the walls and rock
like a mourner
Recite the name
drop the name
oh the name
the *geste*
attention
to the real name of God

Vishnu
Waheguru
Ahura Mazda
Satan
The Light
Father
Raven

Feel the power in the name
Feel it in your socks
Feel the sweat, the juice
of something coming
something is about to happen

Lord
Pangu
Shiva
Wakan Tanka
Zeus
Christ
Mami Wata

Bow down
Bow down
Bend thy head
in praise
in shame
in submission

in admission
in contrition
of the power
the power

Hari
Yahweh
Odin
Vajrasattva
Wicca
Arya Tara
Jupiter

the name
the power
in the name
God.

BACK TO EARTH

Back to Earth, dangerous trip down
our spiritual equilibrium depends
more on Dave Letterman than Siddhartha
or the art teacher whose tits look better than creampuffs
not to be confused with the man on the moon
bumbling around among white padding
        Oh, these drugs are good!
a musical memory racing at 4000 RPMs
on through the lunar night, big daddy
and relived by day, turn by wicked turn
on full throttle just so it rhymes
whatever, 3800, still pretty lucky
considering the times.

SEVEN DAYS A WEEK

They flip by
M T W T F S S
slow down to

seven days in a week
seven notes in a scale
seven seasons in a year
seven fish mounted on the wall
of the mountain diner where
everything tastes so good

walk into Elk Lake Resort, Oregon
at the center of the
campground for a fish burger
and extra fries before
sitting on a porcelain toilet then
flipping my pack up and heading
on; I go but I want to sit by the
lake enjoying outdoors
the sheen off the water
birds in the trees, clean in
my nose, a tall glass of
lemonade homemade served
with a smile
seven days a week.

MAZE OF THORNS

The gods and governors are fools
Guiltily pretending to lead
While stealing Halloween candy jewels
From their own despised baby breed
We turn right left right neither nor
Through a poison needle's kiss
Doesn't it seem we've been here before?
Ouch, I smell my own piss
If it doesn't know the way, why follow the rat?
Who's the fool now? Who's zombie bait?
We can't break out, can't stand pat
Growing darker, soon too late
Somebody's yelling "come on, you're too slow"
So off we go.

THE HOUSE OF EXPERIMENTATION

My fingertips read the braille
on the walls of the insides of boxes in boxes
but I won't tell you what it means
        my hat, it has three corners
        and throw 'em over your shoulder
        gently, gently, down the stream
there's a splinter waiting for every finger
a palming mime on every flank: north, south, and so on
a brass lock with a brass key broken off inside

I should wear a white suit
to push jellybeans into piles as high as your eye
build a new solar system of cosmic dust and gas
at last
nobody will jeer when I spill milk on the radio

a six-headed land serpent
will soon crack its paranoid head up
through the chocolate marble floors
and scream,
        "... two cats in the yard,
        life used to be so hard ..."

my bed is under the sea
I can feel the pressure in my ears

my dick has the bends
even the designs on the pillow cases
are stupid coral wet dreams

I must build up my chest
construct a spicy pot of beans
raise a Babel bookcase for my complete set of 1970's TV
Guides
weave large golden blankets of corn silk
I can
I was there in California when a pixie danced on the beach,
before she cut off her hair
before the silent thugs surrounded me in shadows
before bottles of bitter herb liquor littered the floor with
blank gum wrappers inside
before the sand pit
before you sent me up the river
to the big house

CREDITS

EGO

Etiolate Blues, *Lo Stretto*, May 2012
Coming Out of a Coma, *Literary Yard*, January 2018
Avoiding Mirrors, *Scarlet Leaf Review*, January 2018
Punctuation, *The Electronic Pamphlet*, June 2018
Jumping In and Out of the Mirror, *The Wagon Magazine*, September 2018
Seated After Lunch, *Verse-Virtual*, July 2016
Am I Breathing Gas? *FRIGG Magazine*, 2014
Watching Through a Hole in the Fence, *Scarlet Leaf Review*, July 2016
White Lightning, *The Ugly Writers*, November 2018
Waiting for What in the Bank, *The Ugly Writers*, November 2018

ID

Going to the Edge of the Land, *The Dreaming Machine*, December 2018
One Sweltering Day of the Caronte, *Cecile's Writers Magazine*, May 2018
La Soluzione del Fiammifero (The Match Solution), *Cecile's Writers Magazine*, May 2018
Palmyra Remembered, *Muddy River Poetry Journal*, Fall 2016
Bumming a Third-Class Train, *Nthanda Review*, December 2018

King Hussein and the Blind Man, *The Wagon Magazine*, September 2018
Moving Still, *The Wagon Magazine*, September 2018
Miss America, *Botticelli Magazine*, October 2015

SUPEREGO

Remission of Cancer, *Starving Artist*, July 2016
I Kissed You, *Tower Journal*, Fall 2017
Charlene's Golf Story, *Scarlet Leaf Review*, January 2018
A Century of Accumulation, *Nthanda Review*, December 2018
Me and the Beast, *Nthanda Review*, December 2018
Our War is Over, *The Dreaming Machine*, December 2018
Colonoscopy, *Scarlet Leaf Review*, January 2018
In Court, *The Electronic Pamphlet*, June 2018
Being Chased, *FRIGG Magazine*, 2014
I Am the Urge, *FRIGG Magazine*, 2014

MELANCHOLIA

Good Friend on a Beach, *Verse-Virtual*, July 2016
Death of a Sentient Being, *The Dreaming Machine*, December 2018
Asbestos Factory, *PoeticDiversity*, December 2017
Heirlooms, *Verse-Virtual*, July 2016
I Was Dead, *Scarlet Leaf Review*, January 2018
Call for Prayer, *Verse-Virtual*, December 2016
We Will All Become Vegetarians, *Former People*, 2017
I Repeat Repeat, *Verse-Virtual*, June 2016
On Review, *The Wagon Magazine*, September 2018

PHANTASY

The Koi Are Not Indifferent, *Starving Artist*, July 2016
Waiting for the Bus, *Botticelli Magazine*, October 2015
Look the Other Way, *Strong Verse*, July 2013
Do Food, *The Ugly Writers*, November 2018
Driving My Way, *The Ugly Writers*, November 2018
Weakness, *Ink in Thirds*, February 2017
The Gospel According to Bob, *Starving Artist*, July 2016
The Sun Knows I'm a Fool, *Scarlet Leaf Review*, July 2016
Photos of Food, *Door is a Jar*, July 2017
The Persuaders, *Ibis Head Review*, April 2018
The Name of God, *The Wagon Magazine*, September 2018
Back to Earth, *Revue POST*, May 2018
Seven Days a Week, *Valley Micropress*, November 2017
Maze of Thorns, *Pilcrow & Dagger*, February 2016
The House of Experimentation, *Repurposed Magazine*, September 2017

** some poems slightly edited*

ABOUT THE AUTHOR

E. Martin Pedersen was born in Berkeley, California, then grew up in San Francisco and other towns in northern California. He is a poet, fiction writer, singer-songwriter, and former teacher of English for forty years at the University of Messina. After grad school, Martin left San Francisco, red backpack on his shoulder, set off to see the world, and wound up in Messina, Sicily, where he still lives. He has degrees from the University of the Pacific (Education), San Francisco State University (Creative Arts), and San Jose State University (Folklore, Independent Studies). His academic work earned him the EdPress Feature Award in 1997. His over-350 published poems and short stories have appeared in 140 journals in 17 countries. One haiku was nominated for the Touchstone Awards; one was given the Best Haiku Award from cattails. Martin was Poet of the Week for Poetry Superhighway thrice, and his poem "Gull Eggs" was nominated for the 2023 Best of the Net. Lastly, he is an alumnus of the Community of Writers, where he studied with Anne Lamott, James D. Houston, and Karen Joy Fowler.

Martin's books include: *Bitter Pills* (2020, Cyberwit.net), *Smart Pills* (2021, Cyberwit.net), *Exile's Choice* (2021, Kelsay), plus two books on American music published in Italy. He is currently shopping three novels and three poetry collections. His future writing plans include surrealist and historical novels, themed poetry chapbooks of previously published work, a third haiku book, and songs, including musicals. Martin blogs at emartinpedersenwriter.blogspot.com

In his free time, Martin plays an 1885 banjo and a 1950 ukulele, follows baseball almost obsessively, and, in summers, takes long walks on the Pacific Crest Trail and elsewhere. Martin divides his time between Tracy, California, Furnari, Sicily, and Messina where he lives with his wife Daniela, and his Barbie dog Kiki.

www.ingramcontent.com/pod-product-compliance
Lightning Source LLC
Chambersburg PA
CBHW030308100526
44590CB00012B/561
9781922311580